The son of German immigrant parents who settled in the USA, Dietrich was named after Dietrich Bonhoeffer. He and his wife, Jan, have been involved in church planting in Germany and in Europe for over 37 years. They have three adult children and four grandsons. Dietrich and Jan reside in Wheaton, Illinois.

Dietrich is the author of:

SHIFT: The Road to Level 5 Church Multiplication
The Jesus Model: Planting Churches the Jesus Way
Profound: Twelve Questions That Will Grab Your Heart and Not Let Go

Dedicated to
Jan Carla,
the delight of my eyes.
treasure of my heart,
exquisite gospel practitioner,
my good and beautiful wife.

Dietrich Schindler

BEYOND BELIEF –
FAITH THAT WORKS

AUSTIN MACAULEY PUBLISHERS™

LONDON • CAMBRIDGE • NEW YORK • SHARJAH

A CIP catalogue record for this title is available from the British Library.

ISBN 9781398480438 (Paperback)
ISBN 9781398480445 (ePub e-book)

www.austinmacauley.com

First Published 2023
Austin Macauley Publishers Ltd®
1 Canada Square
Canary Wharf
London
E14 5AA

Melody Raines, your expertise made this good book better.
I am deeply grateful for your editing prowess.

Table of Contents

Foreword

A favorite word used by Christians is the word *gospel*. However, when many Christians use the word, usually they have in mind a not-yet-Christian who seems to need it. Rarely do they think the gospel is for themselves. Truth is, the *gospel* is for all of us, all the time.

Pastor Tim Keller once explained that the gospel isn't simply the ABCs of Christianity, but the A-through-Z. The gospel doesn't just ignite the Christian life; it is the fuel that propels the Christian life forward every day. For the Christian, it is vital to keep the gospel in mind all the time, and even occasionally to preach the gospel to ourselves. The Apostle Paul presents the gospel as the fundamental element of all spiritual growth and Christian maturity, even after one's conversion. *"In the same way,"* he writes, *"the gospel is bearing fruit and growing throughout the whole world—just as it has been doing among you since the day you heard it and truly understood God's grace."* (Colossians 1:6 NIV) Whether a heralded preacher, a healthy Christian or a hardened skeptic—we all need the gospel.

Imagine my delight when my friend Diet Schindler invited me to write the foreword to his newest book, Beyond Belief: Faith That Works. Diet and I met as students while studying in seminary in the early 80s. The churches I've pastored along the way have supported Diet and Jan's missionary work ever since. Diet is a successful church planter, a seasoned pastor-leader, a strategic 'culture-naut' (one who explores culture like an astronaut) and a seminal thinker. For more than three decades Diet has been planting gospel seeds in one of the most challenging contexts in the world—post-Christian Germany. His life motto for years has been, "Five to grow before I go." His dream was to plant five thriving churches on German soil before he died. At last count, Diet has planted six! And knowing Diet as I do, he's likely to add to that number before his time is up!

And speaking of Germany, Reformer Martin Luther, often employed the phrase *simul justus et peccator* to describe his condition as a Christian. The phrase means, "simultaneously justified and sinful." Luther understood what every Christian needs to understand: we are simultaneously saved from sin's *penalty*; but we are equally in need of being saved from sin's *power*. Our salvation from sin's *penalty* occurred in that once-for-all experience, the moment we believed in Christ and were justified in and through Him. Salvation from sin's power is an altogether different experience. It is the daily, ongoing, progressive, and Spirit-empowered experience that is never completed short of glory. It involves plodding, discipline, resilience, along with what the late Eugene Peterson once described as, "a long obedience in the same direction." It is toward this experience that this book speaks so urgently, so eloquently and unapologetically. Spiritual growth is not about working harder—it is about continually reminding ourselves that we are more lost and defective than we ever imagined, but more loved and accepted than we ever dared hope for.

Spiritual growth is about continually rediscovering *"the light of the gospel that displays the glory of Christ."* (2 Cor. 4:4)

I heartily and enthusiastically commend the volume you hold in your hand. Read it to grow your life!

Soli Deo Gloria,
Dr. C. Lee Heyward, Lead Pastor
Elmbrook Church—Brookfield, Wisconsin USA

Introduction

Elvis Presley's knowledge of the Bible was encyclopedic. By the time he was seventeen, he had memorized 1,750 Bible verses. He memorized 350 Bible verses annually, which allowed him to attend summer camp for free for five years in a row.[i] That number of verses exceeds those contained in Genesis, or Job, or in any New Testament book. What a feat!

Despite his vast biblical knowledge, Elvis was shaped more by the drugs, sex, fame, and the alcohol that he consumed than by anything in the Bible.

Theologian Ron Sider has had keen interest in faith and practice in American Christianity for more than half a century. In an interview with *Christianity Today*, Sider speaks of a great disconnect he has noticed:

The heart of the matter is the scandalous failure to live what we preach. The tragedy is that poll after poll by Gallup and Barna show that evangelicals live just like the world. Contrast that with what the New Testament says about what happens when people come to living faith in Christ. There's supposed to be radical transformation in the power of the Holy Spirit. The disconnect between our biblical beliefs and our practice is just, I think, heart-rending.[ii]

For many professing Christians, the gospel is good to know, but of little daily use. In their mind the gospel is what gets them a free ticket to heaven but has little effect on how they live on earth. Their knowledge does not lead to a reordering of their lives. It is knowledge without application.

The difference between Greek and Hebrew learning is foundational. We get our educational system from Greek influence which posits, if we have understood something, we have learned it. On the other hand, Hebrew thinking says only after we have done or applied something have we learned it.

Hebrew pedagogy is the premise behind all of Jesus's teaching. It startles people when they realize that in the Great Commission (Matt 28:18–20) Jesus did not tell us to go and make disciples, "teaching them everything I have commanded you." Rather, he said "teaching them *to obey* everything I have commanded you." The inference is clear: if we haven't applied Jesus' teaching, we haven't learned Jesus's teaching.

Application-based teaching is the goal of the Sermon on the Mount (Matt. 5–7). At the end of Jesus's sermon where he speaks of the two builders who built on two different foundations, what the builders had in common was knowledge. What was distinctive was application, or a lack thereof. "Therefore, everyone who hears these words of mine and puts them into practice is like a wise man who built his house on a rock." (Matt. 7:24)

This book is about believing that behaves, applying what we know of the gospel in our everyday activities. Such experience is more valuable than our next pay-check, more relevant than today's stock report, more personal than our medical history, and more satisfying than our most recent accomplishment. It's about faith that works itself out in our daily living.

Part One
Shelly's Story

The Dent

To say Shelly was one of a kind, would be an understatement. Her sorority sisters knew Shelly as a raucous, hard-partying, fast-driving, tell-it-like-it-is, guy-conquering, foul-mouthed, pretty-good friend. And then the wheels came off. Halfway through her junior year much of the way she related to people changed. Shelly Dixon became a Jesus follower.

Her roommate Jenna caught the first whiff. During one of their weekly battles, Shelly flew off the handle, slammed the door, and left the room. But five minutes later she was back. "Jenna, I'm so sorry. I shouldn't have accused you, and not in that tone. Will you forgive me?" Jenna didn't respond. She didn't know how. This was not the self-righteous Shelly she had always known.

As the weeks went on, the edges wore off. Shelly's crass words, those that stung, slowed to a trickle. Jenna saw Shelly reading her Bible. Instead of partying all night and nursing a hang-over the next morning, Shelly was frequenting a Bible study. She was cleaning up her messes, something that Jenna normally did.

Slowly Shelly's life was being transformed. She loved God's Word and discovered it uncovering her heart, exposing inequities deep within. Her appetite for worship and preaching that was both biblical and practical put her near the front of Community Church's sanctuary on most Sundays. She was even taking notes on the pastor's sermons.

Shelly's heart was still reverberating with joy as she crossed the parking lot to her car after exceptional worship when all hell broke loose. She was just about to squeeze the handle to the driver side door when she became almost physically ill. Someone had put a dent in the door of her brand-new Tesla.

She cursed, then swore up a storm. Blood flushed hot up into her face. "Who is the jerk that did this? I can't believe someone would dent my car like this! They're going to have to pay." On and on she ranted, just like the Shelly of old.

This car meant *everything* to Shelly. She was a 'car guy' ever since she could remember. Her dad pampered his 1972 Dodge Charger coupe driving it only on special occasions such as a birthday or Shelly's graduation. It was the ultimate muscle car, sleek and with 381 horsepower under the hood, a titan of power. Her dad's love of beautiful and strong cars rubbed off on her. Shelly took on a waitressing job just to save enough money for a down payment on her new Tesla (Despite her love of gas fumes, ecology was paramount). It was her dream car. Now it was damaged. The dent in her car's door felt like a stab in Shelly's heart.

The Decision

A cup of coffee sipped in a nearby Starbucks was what she needed right now. Shelly noticed her right hand trembling slightly when she reached for her Java Chip Frappuccino. What was troubling her now went beyond the dent. It had to do with her decision to surrender to Christ and put her faith in him as her Lord and Savior.

"Did I get it right?" was the question that surfaced over and over. It haunted her. Maybe she did not get the words exactly the way they should have been said when she prayed that prayer cementing her decision. She made no sense of the disconnect between her new-found faith and her going off the rails in the church parking lot.

Or deeper still. Perhaps she did not have the right kind of faith. "Did I dig down deep enough? Was my sincerity genuine? Maybe it had to do with some sin that might have escaped me when praying with my small group leader." No, that couldn't be it.

For the first time ever, Shelly felt God lift the massive tonnage from her heart when she prayed that prayer. Something did happen when she made her decision. Her experience told her so. After all, she was all too acquainted with impenetrable shame, the kind that would make a sailor blush if projected onto the screen of a drive-in movie theatre. The cheapness she felt the next day, waking up in a strange bed with a stranger next to her. But the feeling of being diminished washed away after a simple prayer. God was at work, cleansing, healing, renewing.

The decision Shelly made was what others told her made her "born again." Indeed, that was the feeling she had; a freshness and a vibrancy rarely known. She was walking on a cloud. In seconds winter became spring.

But now Shelly was facing a new dilemma: If she had made the best decision of her life, why was it not carrying through in her response to disappointment? Was the new Shelly a retread of the old Shelly? And why couldn't she just let go of what someone had just done to her pride and joy?

She needed to revisit her decision.

Trash Disposal

Shelly was a regular at Common Grounds, the café where Bob and Nancy Stevenson met with about fifteen college kids on Wednesday evenings for Bible study. The format was simple – coffee, prayer, Bible discussion.

They had begun journeying through the Gospel of Mark. Tonight, they were looking at the healing of the paralytic at the beginning of Chapter 2. Someone read the first twelve verses. The man in the story was immobile, stuck to his mat because his legs could not carry him. The group discussion began to center on the obvious: "Like the paralytic, we all have things in our lives that we cannot change."

What was not obvious was Jesus's response to the lame man. Jesus saw the greater need behind the surface need. The man had more than a physical problem. He had a spiritual problem. He was a sinner, a person separated from a life with God. "Son, your sins are forgiven," Jesus said. The parallel made sense: lameness kept the man from walking just as sin prevented him from living a life with God. The antidote to the double malaise was healing and forgiveness; forgiveness being the greater of the two gifts.

Bob, wanting to underscore this truth, reminded the group, "This, in a nutshell, is the gospel. The gospel is the good news of Jesus as our Savior who through his death takes away our sin." A somber stillness settled over them. Shelly, still fresh from her own awakening, responded, "I get it. If sin is filth, then Jesus takes away my filth. He's like my garbage collector, freeing me from the trash that I produced but can't dispose of by myself." The group loved Shelly's analogy. *Yes, that was it,* she thought. Jesus manages our sin so that we can be relieved of our trash and have a personal relationship with God.

Driving home that night in her dented Tesla, Shelly mulled over their discussion. She considered the analogy of Jesus being her personal garbage collector unusually insightful, useful in her interaction with her roommate Jenna. "To be done with what I have done can only be done by the grace of God," flitted through her head. Wow!

Such a pithy saying, and it aptly wraps up the meaning of the gospel. "To be done with what I have done, can only be done by the grace of God." Waste management at its best. Shelly was beginning to understand more of what her decision for Christ meant.

Still, she felt a strange uneasiness. What she understood about the gospel led Shelly to ask, "If the gospel is all about sin management, then why am I still responding to disappointment in ways that produce more trash?"

Common Ground

The question disturbed Shelly for most of the next week, hanging onto her like a low-grade fever. "If Jesus takes away my sin, why do I produce more of it for him to dispose of?" Wanting to talk to someone who had been in the faith longer than she had, she arrived at the café earlier before the Bible study started. Shelly was delighted to see Nancy sitting in the alcove where the group usually met, sipping her cappuccino.

"Hi, Nancy. Can I join you?" Smiling, Nancy motioned for Shelly to sit next to her. As Shelly was sitting down with her own coffee, she asked, "Do you mind if I ask you something?"

"Sure, go ahead." Shelly poured out her frustration at her inability to live a life free of producing trash.

Nancy listened thoughtfully then voiced, "To be honest, Shelly, what you are going through is what we all are experiencing. It's normal. But that's not the problem. The challenge is to know what to do with the sin after we commit it. We need to ask Jesus to forgive us and then to restore our relationship with the Father."

Then Nancy gave an analogy that was helpful. Nancy said, "Sometimes a speck of dust will hit our eye and irritate it. What happens? The eye responds by cleansing itself of the dust. The same goes in our relationship to sin. When we sin, Jesus is the one who frees us from the guilt we have produced. When he takes away the filth, we then can see clearly."

What struck Shelly the most was Nancy's statement, "We are all doing that (sinning, cleansing, repeat). It's normal." The prayers in the Wednesday evening Bible study substantiated Nancy's observation. People were confessing their sin, asking for forgiveness, with specific sins resurfacing from week to week.

Slowly Shelly concluded that forgiveness, as wonderful as it was, was too weak to bring about lasting change.

There had to be something that she was missing in her newfound faith.

What could it be?

Lack Attack

High school was tough for Shelly. During her freshman and sophomore years, she was barely getting the job done, bringing home mostly C grades. She did excel, however, in movie theatres, drive-ins, beach parties, and dancing. Her parents were at their wits end, trying to cajole Shelly into doing even a modicum of study. One day her mother in great frustration blurted out, "Shelly, you need a lack attack! You need to be floored by the consequences of what you're *not* doing. Think about the money you won't make, the opportunities that will pass you by, the guys that won't be interested in you, because you don't care about what is important."

That must have gotten through to her because beginning with her junior year of high school she was Snow White. Shelly woke up out of her apathy-slumber and applied herself. She had the grades to prove it.

This is what she was facing now. Shelly needed a spiritual lack attack. What else would explain the deficiency between faith and practice she was experiencing? What was Shelly lacking? Effort. She needed to apply herself more consistently to being locked into Christ. She needed to surrender more of all areas of her life to the Lord. And she needed to know more of the Bible, much more. If she could master her deficits like she mastered geometry, she was bound to sin less.

Up the Exertion

"That's it! I need to put more effort into following Jesus, and then I'll do better." Shelly targeted her need to expend more effort to become a better Christian. This was her lack attack moment. She started to listen to great podcasts, read books written about in *Relevant* magazine, and go over her sermon notes to check her performance.

Shelly was sobered by an analogy given by the apostle Paul. "Train yourself for godliness." (1 Tim. 4:7) A runner can only win races after putting in the time and effort of training. The same goes for the Christian. Shelly dedicated more of her time to train to become a better Christian.

But the more she tried, the greater her frustration. Everything was aligned – her sincerity, her dedication, her time commitment, her effort. She was doing the work. She wasn't a slacker. "When I put money into a vending machine and press the right button, I receive my selection at the opening at the bottom of the machine. Why, if I'm putting in the currency of effort, am I not getting marked change as a result?" Shelly wanted to know.

The Gospel
According to Shelly

Shelly possessed a partial understanding of the gospel. And that could result in a complete misunderstanding of the gospel.

The stunning message of the good news of Jesus Christ was what captured her heart. She felt like she was walking on a cloud. Then life began to rub up against her conversion experience. She woke up to the rawness of reality. Though the gospel can change everything, much of who she was seemed unaffected by it.

As we look at what Shelly misinterpreted the gospel to be, we may discover ourselves to be in her corner as well.

What was the gospel according to Shelly?

The gospel of compartmentalization

When Shelly put her faith in Jesus as her Lord and Savior, much changed. Even a close friend like Jenna noticed the difference. But then there was the dent. It wasn't any old dent, but a dent in her new Tesla. Why did it upset Shelly so much? Because "it meant everything" to her. Which is another way of speaking of an idol. Often, we think of idols as those manmade images that people bow down to. But an idol can be anything good that becomes the ultimate good. Jesus is then relegated to someone who is good and useful, but there are other things that mean more to us.

Our desks have multiple drawers. What gets put in the top drawer is often what tops the things in the other drawers. We call this compartmentalization, segmenting our lives into units of greater or lesser value.

What is in your "top drawer"? For Shelly it was her new car. The reaction we have when things get out of control will reveal to us what is (or who is) in the top drawer of our lives.

One sure sign that we have something (or someone) of superior value to Jesus is the loss of joy that attends the loss or the diminishing of an idol. Whatever has the power to rob us of joy has power over us. And that is our idol, needing to be toppled.

The gospel of magic words

Shelly was so thrown for a loop by her response to the dent in her new car that she began to call into question how she came to know Jesus. The disconnect between her faith and her behavior in the church parking-lot prompted her to revisit her decision. The possibility that she had gotten it wrong was troubling to her.

Indeed, as all evangelistic campaigns have shown, one can pray the sinner's prayer and still live as a sinner after that. Weaving our eyes through a prayer or mouthing the right words are inadequate if the heart is not connected to the words.

Fortunately for Shelly, she had submitted her heart to Jesus. For to give someone our heart is to give all of ourselves to that person. The unequivocal bonding of mind, will, and emotion to Jesus is the primary thing, and the words we use to cement that bonding are secondary.

The gospel of sin management

It was Bob Stevenson, leading the Bible study along with Nancy, his wife, who spoke of *the gospel in a nutshell*. Jesus does take away our sin. Hallelujah.

But recall the interchange that Wednesday evening. Shelly said, "If sin is filth, then Jesus takes away my filth. He's like my *garbage collector*, freeing me from the trash that I produced but can't dispose of by myself."

Many people come to Jesus when what they are truly seeking is relief. They feel the weight of shame and guilt pressing in on them. They need a disposal service, or a garbage collector, to relieve them of the effects of their sin. Once the trash is taken care of, life can go on pretty much as they want it to.

But Jesus is so much more than waste management. Taking away the refuse is a way of preparing us for beauty in its place. Jesus wants to give us more than what he has taken away.

The gospel of rinse and repeat

When Shelly spoke to Nancy, it was about her dilemma: "If Jesus takes away my sin, why do I produce more of it for him to dispose of?" Nancy gave her the illustration of the eye, which cleanses itself when a speck of dust hits it. The way of forgiveness becomes the pathway to cleansing. Shelly observed that this was indeed the pattern of the others at the Bible study. They would often confess the same sins that they confessed last week. Like using shampoo, it was rinse and repeat.

The gospel of rinse and repeat means that the gospel is strong enough to cleanse us of sin, but too weak to change us from sinning. When we get into a pattern of doom looping, repeatedly asking for forgiveness for the same sins, it's often because we are targeting what we do at the expense of who we have become in Christ. When identity is addressed (who we are), the sinning (what we do) loses its power over us.

The gospel of heightened vigilance

Based on her high school experience, Shelly thought what she needed in her new life with Jesus was a *lack attack*. She needed to redouble her intentionality. She committed herself to greater effort. If she could master her deficits like she mastered geometry, she was bound to sin less.

There is however something insidious about sin. To use the words in the beginning of the Bible, "sin is crouching at the door." (Gen. 4:7) Like a wild animal following us at every good turn, sin is ready to pounce on us to devour us. We will have limited success in subduing sin by being aware of it. But our greatest hedge against sinning is cultivating our joy in the one who is the gospel-Jesus.

A friend of mine was bullied as a child. He hated recess because it meant being exposed to the onslaught of his mean classmate. One day, my friend's father came to pick him up from school. Hand in hand they walked right by the bully, without fear and in no danger of harm. The father's presence made all the difference.

The gospel of the vending machine

Recall the end of Shelly's story. *When I put money into a vending machine and press the right button, I receive my selection at opening at the bottom of the machine. Why, if I'm putting in the currency of effort, am I not getting marked change as a result?* was Shelly's thinking.

God is not a vending machine. The vending machine always gives us something proportionate to what we put into the machine. To treat God this way is to instrumentalize Him, to use Him for our own gain.

Fortunately for us, He will not let that happen. Love is never a means to an end. It is the end. To be loved by the Father is more than we could ever imagine. When He blesses us, it is not with fortuitous events and things. It is with Himself.

Shelly is on a journey of discovering the beauty of the gospel lived out in relationship with Jesus. This is the gospel of joy, and it is the gift given to every Jesus-follower, every day.

We will revisit Shelly and her journey of discovering what it is that needs to change for her to change. But before we re-enter her life, I invite you to contemplate a special piece of artwork. Part of Shelly's dilemma is hidden in a painting that millions of people have seen in the span of more than five hundred years.

Part Two
The Wisdom of Faith

The Mystery Person

Michelangelo's fresco 'The Creation of Adam'
(public domain)

Michelangelo was a thirty-three-year-old sculptor when Pope Julius II commissioned him to decorate his future burial place, the Sistine chapel. The young artist set about his work reluctantly. He was already focused on a marble statue of Moses for Julius's mausoleum when he was asked to paint the ceiling of the chapel. Besides, he saw himself as a sculptor, not as a painter.

Yet Michelangelo painted over three hundred figures on the ceiling, taking us from the creation of the world to the last judgment. The scenes are too much to take in all at once. They have the power to strike awe in our hearts. Seventy feet above us, Michelangelo's work, particularly his famous depiction of God creating Adam rivets us.

In the creation of the first human being, we see two fields of images that starkly contrast each other in both form and meaning. On the left side, we gaze upon a lonely Adam, sitting forlorn in the vacuous created Earth, cold and foreboding. His eyes are sad with a hint of longing. He has no vibrancy, as witnessed by his limp left-hand protruding downward. His body is muscular, yet without energy. We see him in his created state, but in flux.

As we pan to the right, we see God in the act of creating man. In the Genesis creation account, we read of the Spirit of God moving over the waters. Michelangelo shows us in the flowing of God's hair, beard, and garments that the Spirit of God is dynamically active in creating. Surrounding God, we see heaven, where angels press in tightly around the Creator's body. God's right hand, a symbol of strength, is stretched out toward hapless Adam, a resolute index finger about to touch and awaken him to life.

In 1990 an American medical doctor by the name of Frank Lynn Meshberger saw something in the fresco that no one in five hundred years of reflection had noticed. Studying Michelangelo's creation of Adam, Meshberger focused on the outer boundary of the heavenlies, in which God the Creator is the centerpiece. Meshberger theorized that this frame in which heaven is located approximated the shape of the human brain. God himself is resident in the hypothalamus section of the brain where the source of intelligence and creativity are found. Thus, the artist, interpreting the creation of man, postulated that God is creative intelligence through whom we derive our intelligence and creativity.

But Michelangelo embedded an even more profound insight in his masterpiece.

While God is just about to create man, he is cradling a lovely lady under his left arm. Her face glows as she looks toward the man as if to say, "Something's missing, and I will provide it."

Who was Michelangelo depicting in this woman? We know that she is not Eve. The artist documented the creation of Eve in a separate fresco. This is someone else.

Because these are biblical scenes, we need to go to the Bible to discover the identity of the woman under God's arm. In the book of Proverbs, King Solomon, the wisest man who had lived, gives voice to a female character. "The Lord brought me forth at the beginning of his work. Then I was the craftsman at his side. I was filled with delight day by day, rejoicing always in his presence." (Prov. 8: 22–30)

The beautiful woman was not created, but was "brought forth," having been there since before the creation of the universe. She is the personification of wisdom.[iii] Wisdom is mysterious beauty.

The act of creation is God's imprint of beauty on our world. "God saw all that he had made, and it was very good." (Gen. 1: 31). The Hebrew word for good is *tov*. *Tov* has a broad meaning among which is beauty. For example, the initial reason for the existence of trees was for aesthetics. "And the Lord God made all kinds of trees grow out of the ground – trees that were pleasing to the eye (i.e. beautiful) and good for food." (Gen. 2: 9). Returning to Michelangelo's fresco we see wisdom personified as a beautiful woman begetting beauty. Wisdom is beautiful.

In our mad world what we desperately need is something that takes us beyond intelligence. Wisdom provides what intelligence lacks. Wisdom is the ability to know what to do with information from God in a way that allows us to live a meaningful life. Intelligence informs. Wisdom discerns. Intelligence is learning. Wisdom is applying. Intelligence is the fact-of-the-matter. Wisdom is the application of fact that causes flourishing. Wisdom is beautiful in its application of truth.

Wisdom is knowledge of God applied to daily living. For the Hebrew mind it was not simply enough to know things about God. Such knowledge had to be followed up with practical ways of applying truth in loving God and neighbor.

Wisdom as a Way
of Walking

The Bible informs us of how we can apply wisdom to our lives. When Hebrew believers spoke about wisdom, they often used the term *halak*, to walk, to move about, to proceed. It has both a literal and a figurative connotation. The first occurrence of *halak* in the Bible is in Genesis 3:8 when Adam and Eve heard God in the garden in the cool of the day as he was walking. God – perhaps this was Jesus in a pre-incarnate form – was physically meandering with Adam and Eve, enjoying creation. As God walked, Adam and Eve joined him, reveling in community with God and fellowship with him. Life could not get any better than this!

The Old Testament picturesquely refers to a life lived with God as a walk. "When Abram was ninety-nine years old, the Lord appeared to him and said, 'I am God Almighty, walk (*halak*) before me and be blameless." (Gen 17:1)

As we dig deeper, we learn what it means to walk with God, to be a wise person, to live as someone who is uniquely beautiful. The halak-life has five important components attached to it that make it attractive.

Wisdom Is Living in Partnership with God

The halak-life is first and foremost a life lived in concert with God. There is no true abundance when a person goes through life independently of God. An abundant life is lived with God and from God as its source.

To put it another way, the halak-life is the *axiomatic* life. We may not hear the term *axiomatic* often, but we encounter its importance daily. Two plus two equals four is self-evident, or axiomatic. We live with this mathematical concept like the air we breathe.

Here are some more examples of the axiomatic. There is a three-year-old cutting up during the church service. Her father warns her to stop, but she keeps goofing around, distracting others. At one point her father can't take it anymore. In the middle of the service, he gets up, puts his daughter over his shoulder and walks quickly down the main isle of the church. He's about to reach the foyer when the little girl blurts out for all the worshipers to hear, "Pray for me!" Instinctively we know what is self-evident. The little girl is about to be punished.

The guy in the speeding car, who just got his picture taken, knows that in two weeks he'll get a ticket in the mail, along with a very uncomplimentary photo. The kid that cracked open her algebra textbook a half hour before the mid-term exam knows what kind of a grade is probably coming.

A life lived with God is like this too. It is an axiomatic life. King Solomon tell us, "The fear of the Lord is the beginning of wisdom." (Prov 9:10) Our affirming response to the reality of the presence of God is self-evident. To relate to God as God, by reverencing and honoring him leads to wise living.

We also see the axiomatic nature of the Ten Commandments. The Ten Commandments don't begin with the first commandment. They begin with a relationship: "I am the Lord, your God, who brought you out of Egypt, out of a land of slavery." (Ex 20:2) "You certainly will not need any other gods before me, will you?" is the way to understand the point. It is self-evident. The ethics of the Ten Commandments emanate from relating to the God of the covenant. The covenant that God sealed with his people became the basis for the life they were to live.

Wisdom Is Being Led by God

Second, the halak-life is a directed life. The direction comes from outside of ourselves. We don't intuit the good life, rather we are told by God what it is. The Bible frequently uses the word "light" to underscore this truth. "Your word is a lamp to my feet and a light for my path." (Ps. 119:105) Or in the New Testament, we see Jesus saying the same thing about himself, "When Jesus spoke again to the people, he said, 'I am the light of the world. Whoever follows me will never walk in darkness but will have the light of life.'" (John 8:12). Such illumination does not come from within us, rather it is given to us by God.

Wisdom Is the Promise of Blessing

Third, the halak-life has a promise attached to it. The promise is blessing or favor. "Blessed is the man who does not walk (halak) in the counsel of the wicked… but his delight is in the law of the Lord." (Ps. 1:1–2) The promise in Psalm 1 is that of flourishing ("He is like a tree planted by streams of water, which yields it fruit in season and whose leaf does not wither") and God's sovereign attention ("For the Lord watches over the way of the righteous"). And Solomon claims that wisdom also watches over us, "Do not forsake wisdom, and she will protect you; love her, and she will watch over you" (Prov. 4:6).

Wisdom Speaks to Us Personally

Fourth, the halak-life derives its vitality not in life's gratuitous circumstances, but in the meditation on the Word of God: "his delight is in the law of the Lord" (Ps. 1:2). In the same way the beautiful woman in the Sistine Chapel personifies wisdom, the Bible personifies God's revealed truth. The Bible *speaks* as if it were a person. Rightly so, as it comes to us from a personal God. Jesus, interacting with his detractors, said, "You diligently study the Scriptures because you think that by them you possess eternal life. These are the Scriptures that testify [speak] about me" (John 5:39). Or "He who believes in me, as the Scripture *said*, 'From his innermost being will flow rivers of living water.'" (John 7:38, emphasis added).

Wisdom Warns Against Foolishness

Fifth, the halak-life is replete with warnings to those who would trust in themselves and not in God. The Bible refers to such people as fools ("fools despise wisdom and discipline" Prov. 1:7), and as wicked ("Not so the wicked! They are like chaff that the wind blows away" Ps. 1:4). They are like Eli's sons, who, though they as priests had prestigious religious positions, "they had no regard for the Lord." (1 Sam. 2:12)

Wisdom Is Refracted Beauty

Where does the beautiful woman in Michelangelo's fresco get her luster? Her glory is refracted beauty. She is wise because she is at the side of and under the arm of God himself. As the moon reflects the light of the sun, so wisdom reflects the glory of God. Wisdom, intelligence applied, is an attribute of God. The woman as the personification of wisdom is showcasing God.

The halak-life, the way of wisdom, is one of beauty given to any who want God above anything else. But how do we make sense of the beauty of wisdom, a life lived axiomatically, when we look at the New Testament?

The Gospel Is Wisdom-Beauty

The one-time enemy of Christians, the great Hebrew scholar, Paul of Tarsus, lifted the veil of secrecy surrounding the good life. The themes Michelangelo painted, and the Old Testament proclaimed, are declared, and interpreted by Paul.

We do, however, speak a message of *wisdom* among the mature, but not the wisdom of this age or of the rulers of this age, who are coming to nothing. No, we declare God's *wisdom, a mystery* that has been hidden and that God destined for our glory before time began. None of the rulers of this age understood it, for if they had, they would not have crucified the Lord of glory. However, as it is written:

"What no eye has seen,

what no ear has heard,

and what no human mind has conceived,

the things God has prepared for those who love him—

these are the things God has revealed to us by his Spirit.

The Spirit searches all things, even the deep things of God." (1 Cor. 2:6–10, emphasis added)

What are the "deep things" of God? Paul tells us they are the message of wisdom, which is the gospel. In a narrower sense than what we saw in the Old Testament, the New Testament speaks of the wisdom of God as the beauty of the gospel.

The term mystery in the New Testament means something that was once hidden from our understanding but is now revealed to us by God himself. And this revelation is heart-stopping, eye-opening, mind-boggling, beauty.

If the apostle Paul were standing next to us peering up at Michelangelo's creation of Adam, he would say. "Do you see the beautiful woman under God's left arm? Yes, she is stunningly beautiful, but she is more than that. Her beauty is the beauty of wisdom, and her wisdom is that of the gospel of God, which is now revealed to us in Jesus Christ."

The creator of the world, Jesus Christ, is the savior of the world. He is the beauty of the mystery of God.

Natural-Supernatural Wisdom

Natural-Supernatural – joining these two concepts together seems to us to be an oxymoron. Like boneless ribs, a good beating, or a numb feeling, *natural-supernatural* sounds self-contradictory. Either something is natural and thus pertains to what is part of human living, or it is *super*natural and is above the plane of human living. The supernatural is unlimited, eternal, all-powerful, and holy. The natural by contrast is limited, weak, and unholy. Thus, to wed natural with supernatural is like attempting to mix oil with water. It just doesn't work. The two are of vastly different consistencies, disallowing any cohesion whatsoever.

We need an oxymoronic perspective. So much of Christian thinking on the surface seems to be logically inconsistent, yet it forms the bedrock of our faith. The apostle Paul categorically states this when he writes, "We preach Christ crucified." (1 Cor. 1:23). The gospel presents us with harmonic dissonance. On the one side we proclaim Christ, who is the Son of God, the Savior of the world, the sinless and holy second person of the Trinity. And on the other side we preach Christ *crucified*. A crucified person was legally culpable, having done something so egregious as to deserve death, even execution on a cross. A crucified Christ was as abhorrent to first-century hearers as it is to twenty-first century post-moderns. When people heard Paul proclaiming such a "gospel" (literally "good news"), they either rejected it outright as nonsense or it became to them a stumbling block to faith (ibid). Yet Paul says of this oxymoronic gospel that it forms both the power and the wisdom of God (1 Cor. 1:24). There is a fullness of meaning that is found only in its seemingly self-contradictory expression.

This is the stuff that rocked Martin Luther to the core. Wanting to justify himself before God, Luther wore himself out trying. Flagellations, long bouts of fasting, purposefully exposing himself to the elements, and confession of sin to the point of soul exhaustion led Luther to become angrier with God rather than drawn to him in love. It was the sudden realization, while studying Galatians and Romans, that God's justice is revealed in the opposite of justice in the justification of sinners that ultimately threw Luther into the arms of Christ.

God is known through what is contrary. He is known in a hidden way. God's invisible attributes are revealed in suffering and in the cross – glory in shame, wisdom in folly, power in weakness, victory in defeat. God is known through the message of the cross. The theology of the cross stems from Luther's understanding of righteousness and justification. Luther's great realization was that God justified sinners. God declares those who are unjust to be just. And Luther realized that this being so, human notions of justice could never lead us to understand God's justice.[iv]

Angels Seeking the
Sight of the Oxymoronic

Paul preached such a self-contradictory gospel, and Peter says, "Angels long to look into these things" (1 Peter 1:12). Angels are created beings, inhabiting the supernatural realm, living in the presence of God to do his bidding. They have no need to eat or sleep and do not age. They move freely through physical barriers and have enormous power granted to them by God himself. But before creation, angels by experience only knew heaven.

We cannot fully imagine how eagerly angelic beings longed to peer into the natural-supernatural estate of the sufferings of Christ. The word Peter uses for *long* means intense longing. In some instances, this word is used for lust (see Matt. 5:28; James 4:1; Col. 3:5). The angels knew the sovereign Christ as their omnipotent Lord and Creator. But they had yet to see him in a natural state – the state of weakness and suffering, which he willingly brought upon himself to free sinners from their sin and alienation from God. To the angels, this was absolutely out of their world, absolutely astounding, absolutely horrifying, absolutely wonderful, and absolutely beautiful! Angels bowed down in worship before Christ all-powerful, and they longed greatly to peer into the mystery of the hyphen: the natural – supernatural Lord Jesus Christ.

The incarnation is God in his limitlessness becoming human, and thus consigning himself to limitation. The incarnation is an oxymoron. The apostle Paul refers to this in Philippians 2 as the emptying. Christ, the Son of God, the second person of the Godhead, relinquishes his endemic right to honor and glory. He makes himself vulnerable, weak, and able to be victimized – for our sake. We strain to wrap our minds around such condescension, reeling from it. Like peering over the outside balustrade at the top of the Eifel tower, feeling it sway as we look down, we get dizzy, needing to hold on to the railing for fear of losing our balance. Such is the utter incomprehensible nature of the incarnation of God in Jesus Christ.

As seminary professor Jack Miller and pastor Timothy Keller have taught us, the gospel states that we are greater sinners than we would dare to admit, but more loved by God than we could dream in our wildest dreams. Recently I found myself trying to wrap my mind around this incomprehensible gospel of Jesus Christ. I concluded that could very well lead to insanity, just to think that God would go to such depths to love me, who was in such deep mire.

We do well to stand in awe of the oxymoronic natural-supernatural blended natures of Jesus Christ.

Living in the Overlap

Jesus's disciples were fascinated with Jesus and his prayer life. So enthralled were they by his unusual dialogue with the Father that they asked Jesus to teach them to pray as he prayed. Jesus answered with what we commonly refer to as "the Lord's prayer." What was the Lord's prayer became the disciples' prayer. In it the two worlds in which we as disciples of Jesus live become apparent. The emphasis is on the presence and the power of the Father *in heaven* to be manifest among us *on earth*: "Thy kingdom come. Thy will be done on earth as it is in heaven." Tom Wright comments on the focus of this prayer:

We are called to live at the overlap both of heaven and earth – the earth that has yet to be fully redeemed as one day it will – and of God's future in this world's present. We are caught on a small island near the point where these tectonic plates, heaven and earth, future and present, are scrunching themselves together. Be ready for earthquakes.[v]

It is significant to note that the term – heaven – in the Lord's prayer in our English translations is singular, but the word in the Greek is plural: "in the heavens." How is the will of God to be done on earth as it is being done *in the heavens*? First-century Jewish thinking helps us here. Jewish believers conceived of three distinct spheres. The first heaven was between the earth and the clouds. The second heaven was between the clouds and the stars. The third heaven was God's reality beyond the stars in a place called heaven. God, who is at home in all the heavens, in all the spheres, is very near to us in our daily living.

We have seen that wisdom is a new kind of living, a beautiful manner of living (halak) in concert with the living God. But we have seen that it is more than simply a new lifestyle. It is the gospel itself.

This is where we return to Shelly. Like Shelly, we are confronted with the stark reality of daily life. How do we not only believe Jesus to be the gospel, the good news, beauty in all of his glory, but also live it out – axiomatically?

Part Three
Faith at Work –
Belief That Behaves

Another term for what I am attempting to describe concerning walking in wisdom is the kingdom of God. When Jesus came preaching, his message was the good news of the kingdom of God. He proclaimed it in the third person, but meant himself in the first person, for he was the king of the kingdom.

A kingdom then is the realm in which the king has his way. In the word kingdom we get a hint of what it is. "Dom" at the end of kingdom is a shortened form for dome or dominion. A cathedral is sometimes referred to as a dome. Under the cupola of an old cathedral, we are reminded of where we are. We are in the Domus Dei, in the house of God. Like the tabernacle and the temple in the Old Testament, the dome was to depict life lived in another reality, the reality of being in the very presence of God.

Jesus used an architectural term in John 15 to say the same thing. "If a man remains ([or abides] in me and I in him, he will bear much fruit" (John 15:5). When we are at home in Jesus and Jesus is at home in us, this indwelling will necessarily produce abundant nourishment – much fruit. This is living self-evidently.

Essentially a life lived from God is a life drawn from him as our source. The analogy of water as it sustains our lives is often used it the Bible.

In Genesis 26 Isaac and his servants are constantly searching for water. Their fights with Abimelech's servants over wells show us how treasured water was in that agrarian culture. To deprive a herdsman of water was to destroy his wealth. Without water, the sheep or cattle would die and so would the livelihood of the owner. Abimelech's shepherds closed off the wells that were once dug by Abraham, thereby expelling Isaac and his shepherds from the land.

We read that Isaac moved on from there and dug another well, and no one quarreled over it. He named it Rehoboth [meaning "room"] saying, "Now the Lord has given us room and we will flourish in the land." (Gen. 26:22). The water source underneath the fields became the means by which what was on the fields – animals, crops, and people – would flourish. Just as 2+2=4, it becomes self-evident, an undisputed law, that abundance will be the result.

Misconceptions of being a Christian

Mark Twain was once asked about his definition of church. He replied, "A church is a good person telling good people how to be good." Twain's remark is, of course, a common assumption that is quite wrong. According to Twain, the church is a moral factory. Its foreman, the pastor, is forming good material, his parishioners, into better material. To be a morally good person is not the exclusive domain of Christianity. We all know of non-Christians who are much better people than many Christians, or adherents of other religions who outshine followers of Jesus.

Upbringing and education can be good influences on both children and students. They can turn them into honest, caring, loving, hard-working adults. But Christianity is not an educational system (despite many of us having attended Sunday *school*).

The Connected Life

The core of Christian living goes beyond morality. Being a Christian is essentially tethered to what makes a Christian a Christian, namely, Christ. The person of Christ and the deeds

57

of Christ *ontologically connected* to the Christian, make the Christian who she or he is.

Ontology is the doctrine of life or being. The Christian's life with God is a result of God's life being imparted to her through Jesus. She may be physically alive like the next person on her street, but in terms of being a Christian, that life comes from partaking in the life of Christ.

Saint Paul says it well in his epistle to the Ephesians. "As for you, *you were dead* in your transgressions and sins, in which you used to live when you followed the ways of this world. But because of his great love for us, God, who is rich in mercy, *made us alive with Christ*" (Eph. 2:1, 5, emphasis added). We were once 'dead men walking.' Dead people make it on the cover of Vogue, are seen at beauty pageants, and are members of ethics committees. We shouldn't be fooled by appearances.

No, in the Christian there is something at work that is as vibrant as an underground river. This river is the very person, the very life of God. And because it is God's life resident in us, it is indestructible, resurrection-type life. What Paul is getting at here is a *new quality* of life that is at the core of being a Christian. This is not an add-on or something cosmetic. It is take-your-breath-away, electrifying vibrancy. It is Life with a capital L. It will leave us numb with ecstasy, stupefied by its reality, addicted to its beauty. Why? Because it's God. God, resident within us! Now, sit down in your favorite chair and let that sink in for the next hour.

There are some questions that we can answer with the word sometimes. But there are other questions where responding with the word *sometimes* is incredible. "Do you like to eat vanilla ice cream?" To that you might respond,

"Sometimes." But what if I were to ask if you were born in Milwaukee, Wisconsin, and you were to answer, *"Sometimes"*? That would be incredible, unbelievable. Either you were born in Milwaukee (and love brats) or you weren't. The same can be said of a Christian. "Are you a Christian?" cannot be answered with "Sometimes."

If we miss this new life given to us by God, we will miss what it means to live a beautiful life. This is not morality tacked onto morbidity. This is life *emanating* from life, life overflowing unto life lived out axiomatically.

Further down in Ephesians 2, Paul writes, "For we are God's workmanship, created in Christ Jesus to do good works, which God prepared in advance for us to do." (Eph. 2:10). The word for "workmanship" in the original language is the word from which we derive *poem*. A poem is a written work of art. Paul is saying we are God's work of art. He has given spiritual life to us. For what reason? "To do good works which God prepared in advance for us to do." Notice again, the good works that we are to do are tied to the first work that God has done – the work of restoring us from death to life.

The Christian life is the displaced life. Remember seventh-grade science class? The teacher filled a glass with water. He asked us how to empty the water without turning over the glass. We were stuck. (Okay, I'll speak for myself.) Then he placed some stones into the water glass. We witnessed the water in the glass flowing out from the top. The stones had a greater density than that of the water, so the stones displaced the water.

When we are given a new life, a life from above (John 3:7), it takes on a greater density than what was previously within us – our old life lived around the self. The new life produces new life. These are the good works that God has prepared for us to do. But they can only be done axiomatically, out of the reservoir of that which was given to us by God – new life in Christ.

Becoming Proficient

The gospel is the life of Christ transmitted into our lives – at great cost to him. We have seen that when Christ lives in us, we are not merely morally good people. A supernatural life enables us to live the life of God naturally in our world, out of which appears goodness.

The question that we are left with is that of application. So how do we live such a beautiful life – self-evidently?

Let's take a look at some of those who lived it before our time.

Madame Guyon was a seventeenth century aristocrat who lived moment by moment in the presence of Christ. She did this despite great injustices. Jeanne Guyon, imprisoned, penniless, abandoned by family and friends, lived serenely without bitterness or malice in freeing communion with Jesus. Her spiritual director asked her to write about the secret of the vibrancy of her inner life. In her book *Experiencing the Depths of Jesus Christ*, she describes praying the Scriptures and beholding the Lord (the stilled mind contemplating the beauty of Christ) as her self-evident Christian life.

Brother Lawrence was an eighteen-year-old French soldier when he, having experienced the gospel of God, covenanted to become a lay brother in the order of the

Carmelites in Paris in 1666. For the next forty years of his life, he served his fellow monks by cooking, washing pots, pans, plates, and silverware in the kitchen of the monastery.

What was unusual about Lawrence was not his education, for he was but a simple man. What made him stand out was his life lived with God in the very ordinary circumstances of life, mostly in the kitchen. Those who knew him well testified that he was a wholly consecrated man whose fervor for Jesus was the same in corporate worship as it was in the busyness of work. He lived his life practicing the presence of Christ, living in the very center of the gospel. So profound was this practice that heads of state as well as ecclesiastical elite sought his counsel and his intercession.

My wife gave me a slim volume on the life and words of Brother Lawrence when we were dating in college years. I have been so smitten by this man's life that I try to reread "The Practice of the Presence of God" annually.

In the last century, Frank Laubach, gave us another example of what it looks like to live self-evidently. Laubach, a Columbia University Ph.D., was a missionary and educator in the Philippines in the 1940s and 50s. Laubach is the only missionary that has been depicted on a US postal stamp. He was known as "the Apostle to the Illiterates" for his method of teaching reading that helped millions of people become readers.

Laubach applied with the idea of being in continual conscious communion with God in every moment of every day. He wrote a devotional pamphlet entitled "The Game with Minutes" in which he described his habit of keeping God at the center of his mind one second of every minute of the day. He would ride public transportation, silently pray for those around him, then observe their response. Frank Laubach, as Brother Lawrence before him, learned to be continually in God's presence through trial and error.

Should we want to live out the beauty of the gospel axiomatically, it will largely have to do with spiritual disciplines. And as with all disciplines, there are many failed attempts – but along the way, some significant breakthroughs.

When the disciples caught Jesus in prayer, they wanted that for themselves. "Teach us to pray" (Luke 11:1), they asked him. Then Jesus said, "When you pray, say: Father, hallowed be your name, your kingdom come, your will be done on earth as it is in heaven."

The first three of the six petitions in the Lord's Prayer have to do with the Father. Notice, they are all imperatives, as if to say, "Father, I command you, that your name should be hallowed (set apart, sanctified). I command you that your kingdom should come. I command you that your will should be done on earth as it is in heaven." How crazy is that! Commanding God. But this is what Jesus taught us to do.

Have you ever consciously prayed the first three petitions as imperatives to the Father hundreds of times a day? Why not? And why not make them personal, "Father, I command you, that your name be hallowed *in my life today*"? It can be done, and it waits to be done by those of us living from within to outside of us, axiomatically.

Practicing the Presence with GRACE

Another axiomatical spiritual discipline is with an acrostic of the word GRACE.

Dallas Willard once said, "grace is not opposed to effort, it is opposed to earning."[vi] What would it mean to work out our salvation, to work out grace in our lives, daily?

We begin with our premise that the Christian life is life derived from God. The life we as followers of Jesus live, is the life which flows from his life. Jesus' living flows over into our living.

So we must ask ourselves, how does God show his life in our world? As we see God in action, we will desire to act in accord with him.

Let's consider five aspects of God's character that are related in the ways he relates to this world. God is generous, righteous, aiding those in need, changing his followers into Christ's likeness, and evangelistic. In other words, God is GRACE – filled, longing that we will be filled by his grace.

Gospel Life	Context	Means of Action	Opposite
Generosity	Lack	Giving	Tightfistedness
Righteousness	Shame	Comforting	Blame
Aid (service)	Helplessness	Doing	Passivity
Change	Irritation	Being	Self-Satisfaction
Evangelism	Distance	Going	Security

Generosity

God is generous. He gave us this world, his son, and life lived with him – the gospel. Psalm 23 could rightly be understood as the psalm of generosity, "The Lord is my shepherd, I shall not be in want (i.e., I have no lack)." The psalmist, King David, goes on to describe life lived under our shepherd God, who provides generously for us. He provides us with sustenance, inner restoration, guidance, protection, peace, comfort, fullness, goodness, love, and a forever home with him.

As God is generous, his people emulate him by showing generosity.

If anyone is poor among your fellow Israelites in any of the towns of the land the Lord your God is giving you, do not be hard-hearted or tight-fisted toward them. Rather, be openhanded and freely lend them whatever they need. Be careful not to harbor this wicked thought: "The seventh year, the year for cancelling debts, is near," so that you do not show ill will toward the needy among your fellow Israelites and give them nothing. They may then appeal to the Lord against you, and you will be found guilty of sin. Give generously to them and do so without a grudging heart; then because of this the Lord your God will bless you in all your work and in everything you put your hand to. There will always be poor people in the land. Therefore, I command you to be openhanded toward your fellow Israelites who are poor and needy in your land.

(Deut. 15: 7–11)

As followers of Jesus, we are like artesian wells. We have received from the overflow of God's blessing and can thus pass on some of that blessing to others. The apostle Paul asks two rhetorical questions, "What do you have that you did not receive (Answer: nothing). And if you did receive it, why do you boast as though you did not?" (Answer: pride)

(1 Cor. 4:7)

We are stewards of the good things God has entrusted to us to manage them according to his heart. Our bank account is not ours. It's his. Our car, home, time – they don't really belong to us. They are his given to us both to enjoy and to deploy.

How do we become people of generosity? By becoming students of lack. We pray the kingdom prayer: "Jesus, my king, I want to expand your kingdom today." Jesus answers such prayer. He will begin to surface inequity, need, even poverty within our view. Some of it might be monetary lack, some might be lack of love or affection. We will not alleviate all lack, but certainly we will alleviate some of it through the means afforded us by God.

When my wife and I first got married, I was in seminary, and we were on welfare. Despite both of us working part-time jobs, and living in a trailer, we were barely making ends meet. Our parents would regularly drop by with groceries, or people from our church would donate clothes for our two small children.

In those days I would sometimes do pulpit supply to earn a little bit to help us out. One Sunday morning I preached in a small, struggling church. After I gave the message, I sat down on the front row. It was time for the offering. I think I had eleven dollars in my wallet. The usher, plate in hand, held it out in front of me. I was caught off guard. My wallet was out quickly, but as I went for the lone dollar, I inadvertently clasped the ten-dollar bill with it as well. Honestly, I was mortified. Ten bucks was a week's groceries, and it was the honorarium that day. This was about to become a monetarily no-win situation. There in the offering plate were my eleven dollars. I recall both the usher and I were momentarily stunned. In a church of thirty people the usher was not accustomed to seeing such opulence, never mind by the guest preacher. But there was no going back.

At the end of the meeting, as people were filing out of the service and thanking me for my message, the usher came up to me and pulled me aside. He pressed the ten dollars that I had let fall into the offering plate into my hand and quietly said, "Here, I don't think you wanted to do this." I was dumbfoundedly grateful was for a gesture of such great generosity!

What keeps us from being generous in our living is tightfistedness, which is a form of heart disease. Stinginess in the face of obvious need comes from hardheartedness. Becoming hard of heart begins with being emotionally unmoved by the plight of others. I purposely wrote *becoming*. Hardness of heart is learned behavior. Callousness builds up that effectively suppresses empathy.

But what we have learned can be unlearned. This is part of being a disciple, a student of Jesus. We come to him and say, "Lord, you see my callousness, my lack of empathy and non-compassion toward neediness. I am so different than you are. Teach me your way. Soften my heart. Do this so that I may become a conduit of your joy in giving to those in need." And as he softens our hearts, we open our hands.

Righteous

God is generous, and God is righteous. Another word for righteous is just. God's justice restores what is not morally right to what is right.

There are two sides to justice: one is legal, and one is personal. Injustice leads to guilt and shame. But God, as the God of righteousness who takes the offence upon himself, frees us from both guilt and shame. "He has told you, O man, what is good; and what does the Lord require of you but to do justice, and to love kindness, and to walk (*halak*) humbly with your God?"

(Micah 6:8).

The admonition given to us by the prophet Micah is to *do* justice (not just to think it). How do we live this out? We begin with the kingdom-prayer: "Jesus, my king, I want to expand your kingdom today." Then we open our eyes and our hearts to injustice around us.

The gospel addresses both our loss of legal standing before God (our guilt) and the loss of self-esteem (our shame). Because the gospel has restored us, we will undergird and support societal efforts to overcome inequity, or injustice. But we will also aim to free people from shame or dishonor.

My parents were born and raised in Germany, where a whole nation of people suffered under the burden of shame after World War II. My parents met and married after the war in the mid-1950s. With very few resources and little English language ability, they immigrated to Milwaukee, Wisconsin, in 1955. My father, who was trained as a machinist and as an electrician, struggled to find work. At that time Milwaukee was heavily unionized. It was an anomaly to find non-union work. My dad started out working as an electrician for a non-union shop. At night union electricians attempting to defeat the non-union shops, would at times rip apart the work done that day by non-union guys like my father.

I remember my father painfully relating to us kids how he was maligned by union guys calling him a Nazi. You cannot imagine how hurtful that was to my father. They were shaming and blaming him, calling him something that he was not. Shame always seeks to damage our identity, and as such goes deeper than legal injustice. Shame eats away at our sense of wholeness and honor. Shame is the power to diminish a person.

How do we live this out? We begin with the kingdom prayer: "Jesus, my king, I want to expand your kingdom today." Then we open our eyes and our hearts to the injustice around us.

When we pray the kingdom prayer, we will be on the lookout for people around us who have been diminished. We will seek to be Jesus to them, living as the Holy Spirit functions within us to comfort the shamed. To comfort is to share in someone's pain, to take it upon ourselves, to come along side those who are hurting. It is not giving advice but being sorrowful together. Shame aims to put down, but justice will always raise up the downtrodden.

Aid

God is generous, God is righteous, and God comes to our aid. He serves us.

When I was a kid, kindergarten was more of a shaping than it was a knowledge factory. "Don't hit one another. Take turns. Help clean up. Put on your smock before you paint. No talking during nap time. Put your coat on before you go out to play." And more to home, *"Dietrich, stop pulling Joanne's hair!"*

Have you ever considered Jesus as a kindergarten teacher? If you look at the Gospels, it's an almost inescapable conclusion. The disciples were in kindergarten. They were being taught by Jesus how to behave. At one point, toward the end of his life on Earth, when Jesus was on a collision course with the cross, the kindergarten kids were fighting about who was teacher's pet. Two of them wanted to have their desks right next to the teacher's desk. The other kids got wind of it and got into a fight.

Like all good kindergarten teachers, Jesus intervened. He gave the whole class a lesson on how he expected them to behave. They were to serve one another, just as he came to serve them (more on this in Mark 10).

In God's lesson plan for his children, the first lesson is service. It is learning to behave the way Jesus behaved. Sometimes, like children, we – like the disciples in kindergarten – secretly ask ourselves, "What do I get of this? What's in it for me if I trust in Jesus?" But teacher Jesus flips the question on its head and says, "What's in it for others, now that you are my pupils?"

Serving is the show-and-tell of kindergarten. It lets people in need see, touch, and feel what the kids of the kingdom of God are like.

Living axiomatically is about aiding or serving those who need help. It is being the extension of God's hands, eyes, feet, and mind. God longs to touch the helpless ones of this world mediately through us. And like kindergarteners, we can all learn to be helpers.

If there is a master helper in my world, it is my wife Jan. I know no one who is more ready to jump to the aid of the helpless than she is. A woman in our neighborhood is dying of cancer. She's in a wheelchair and very limited in what she can do. Let's call her Frau Schmidt. If Frau Schmidt needs to get her hair cut, Jan will push her in her wheelchair around our village to get to the hairdresser. When Frau Schmidt is low on groceries or the staples, Jan will shop for her. After Frau Schmidt uses the pot next to her bed to do her duty, it is Jan who empties and cleans the pot.

The other day the phone rang at 5:30 a.m. It was Frau Schmidt calling. She was lying on the floor, having slipped off her wheelchair, and couldn't get up. Who does Frau Schmidt call at 5:30 in the morning after sitting on the floor for an hour? Jan. Then Jan says to her husband who is still in his bathrobe, "Come on, we've got to go over and help her get back into bed."

When Frau Schmidt saw me in my bathrobe, she laughed and said I looked like Fred Astaire. (Despite not being able to dance, I took that as a compliment.) To be honest, I haven't really progressed much beyond kindergarten. I'm still learning, learning from my wife Jan, what it's like to be Jesus to others.

Sometimes I'm more inclined toward the opposite of service – passivity. When I'm immobile after seeing someone in need, I am opposing God and what he wants to accomplish. Who would want to do that?

But when I pray the kingdom prayer, "Jesus, my king, I want to expand your kingdom today," I begin to pick up on people's needs and come to their aid with the resources I have.

Change

But there's still more to being grace-filled, to living out our salvation. There is the challenge not to remain the person we have become. God is always opposed to the status quo. The status quo for most people, and I am like most people, is self-satisfaction. Sure, I'm all for change, but in others.

Sometimes when people show up at my birthday parties and attempt to congratulate me, they are at a loss for words. Sheepishly with a tinge of embarrassment they say, "Congratulations, Dietrich! Stay the same as you are." Now, when the lovely Jan hears that, she hits the roof and says, "No, he shouldn't stay the same. He needs to change!" That's when we shuffle off to the table with the cake on it.

Who wants change? God does. The normal word for a Christian in the New Testament is not *Christian* (used only three times in the entire Bible, mostly negatively) but *disciple* (used more than three hundred times). What is a disciple? A disciple is a student. What does a student do? He or she learns from the teacher. In our case, we learn from Jesus how to be like him in our character. (The fruit of the Spirit is the fruit of Jesus.)

Paul's writing on the fruit of the Spirit (Gal 5:22–23) challenges us to be changed. There we read of nine qualities that God possesses with absolute perfection that are underdeveloped in us: love, joy, peace, patience, kindness, goodness, faithfulness, gentleness, and self-control.

For the most part, Jesus teaches us how to become like him situationally and not in a classroom. The best way to notice where Jesus wants to change us, is to be attentive to what irritates us. Often when someone criticizes us, for example, we push back. But we lean in. Criticism is a divine gift that helps us put our finger on what needs to be changed.

If you are not among the faint of heart, let me challenge you with the following assignment. In the next week, go to three people in your life who know you well and ask each one the same question: "If you were God and you had the power to change one thing about who I am, what would that be?" Brace yourself. Their answers will all three probably go in the same direction. Whatever they say, respond with "Thank you. I know it took great courage to tell me this." And then you can partner with Jesus as your teacher to grow in that one area of character development.

For the more timid among us, here is a less confrontational assignment. Read 1 Corinthians 13:4–7 out loud:

Love is patient, love is kind. It does not envy, it does not boast, it is not proud. It does not dishonor others, it is not self-seeking, it is not easily angered, it keeps no record of wrongs. Love does not delight in evil but rejoices with the truth. It always protects, always trusts, always hopes, always perseveres.

Then read it again aloud, but this time substitute your name for the word *love*. Ask yourself, "In this self-description, what lines up *least* with who I am?" When you have it, then you have located your personal growth issue. Remember, it is not good to stay the kind of person you have become. God wants to change you, to make you more like Jesus.

Evangelism

I have been an avid coin collector since I was seven years old, having been infected with the numismatic virus by my father. As kids, my friends and I rode our bikes a couple of blocks down the road to the pharmacy or the grocery store. We were loaded with a few rolls of Lincoln cents or, if we happened to be wealthy that day, with Jefferson nickels. We exchanged our rolls for new rolls of coins, went outside and rifled through the new rolls looking for collectable dates. We kept the valuable coins, replacing them with ordinary coinage and went back to the cashier to do the same thing all over again. We never spent a valuable coin. A collectable coin was always saved from further circulation, often pressed in to an empty slot into our Whitman coin folder.

Followers of Jesus are often like sought-after coins. When they get found, they are taken out of circulation. And those valuable coins, those in mint state that have never been circulated, are often enclosed in plastic holders (sometimes referred to as slabs). Thus, the collector can gaze upon the luster and beauty of his coins without damaging them.

Too many followers of Jesus have taken themselves out of circulation. They no longer rub up against other coins as they circulate from hand to hand.

There's also a maritime saying that expresses this idea. "A ship is safe in the harbor, but that's not what ships were made for." A Christian is safe in his or her Christian group/church/community, but that's not what the Christian was saved for!

The word evangelize is derived from the Greek word, *euanngelion* – "good news." It is good news because something incredibly beautiful has just occurred: Someone has raised me from the dead.

Suppose you had just won, against all odds, the lottery – 25 million dollars. The first thing you would feel compelled to do is to tell someone (a lawyer, a banker, your spouse). Well, guess what? Against all odds, you were given life eternal, here and now. That's more than hitting the jackpot. When our lives are transformed by the good news, we want others' lives to be transformed too.

Jesus said, we should go and tell the good news, which is the person and deeds of Jesus, powerful to upend, to all people. "Go into all the world and preach the good news to all creation" (Mark 16:16).

The kingdom prayer will compel us to want to tell. "Jesus, my king, I want to expand your kingdom today." What is the context in which we speak the good news to others? It is in response to their bad news. Bad news is the soil for good news.

The good news in the bad news is, "There is a God who has been where you are. There is a king who took upon himself the worst of you. There is a Helper for those who cannot help themselves. There is Someone who can even heal good people of their self-goodness. Let me tell you about him because I have been transformed by him."

Part Four
Shelly's Story Revisited

Shelly found herself in the second great awakening of her Christian life. The first great awakening was during her junior year in college when she became a Jesus follower. She experienced so much that testified to her aliveness: freedom from guilt, recovery from shame, a refocusing from self to others.

But it was the dent in her new Tesla, the stab in her heart that became the fulcrum point of true transformation for Shelly, her second great awaking to the beauty of the gospel. That car meant everything to her. And when something means everything, it becomes a god. The injury to her car was violence to her soul. The shaking hand at the Starbucks was proof that she had derailed (not to mention her profuse swearing in the church parking lot).

Her default modus to assuage her pain was a concoction made up of forgiveness and effort. But as she learned, forgiveness may wipe the slate clean, but it had no real inert power to empower lasting change. Like her friends at the Bible study at Common Grounds, she became a repeat offender – sinning, asking for forgiveness, sinning again.

Shelly fell back on what had worked in her high school days: effort. She had her lack attack, but the effects wore off with time.

What brought about Shelly's second great awakening was discovering that the gospel was much, much more than sin management or being a better person. The gospel, the person of Jesus the king, became to her the beauty she had always longed for. Her affection for Jesus *displaced* her appetite for lesser things. She began to consciously live in daily communion with her Love. He in turn affected her desires, which in turn rewired her behavior. Shelly was learning to live a life of integrity, where her outer world was the same as her inner world. She was working out her salvation, a beautiful life.

One Sunday morning at Community Church the worship leader led the congregation in an old hymn. Shelly had never heard it before.

> She loved the first verse:
> Come thou fount of every blessing
> Tune my heart to sing thy grace
> Streams of mercy never ceasing
> Call for songs of loudest praise
> Teach me some melodious sonnet
> Sung by flaming tongues above
> I'll praise the mount I'm fixed upon it
> Mount of thy redeeming love[vii]

Why did she like the first stanza so? Because it was axiomatic in its thrust. Jesus was the first cause, the "fount of every blessing." The gospel, the person of Jesus, was the underground current coming up and overflowing blessing to affect blessing.

But then she recoiled when the last stanza was sung:

O to grace how great a debtor daily I'm constrained to be!
Let thy goodness like a fetter, bind my wandering heart to thee
Prone to wander Lord I feel it, prone to leave the God I love
Here's my heart, O take and seal it, seal it for thy courts above

"Prone to wander Lord I feel it, prone to leave the God I love." No, she couldn't with good conscience sing that. It wasn't in her heart of hearts. No, she was so in love with Jesus, that to entertain the thought of leaving him made her physically sick.

Physically ill, that's what I felt when I discovered my Tesla was dented, she thought. *But now that my affection is toward Jesus, he means everything to me.* It was in that moment of insight that she knew, *Jesus is the center of my heart and all else flows out from living in communion with him.* Jesus, the gospel, filled her with joy.

Later that day, she talked to her roommate, Jenna, about what she was thinking. They had often spoken of relationships and of what kind of men they were attracted to. "Jenna, imagine marrying a guy, who at the altar says to you, 'Prone to wander, Jenna, bride I feel it, prone to leave the wife I love'! You'd run out of the church and leave him there. I know I would."

Jenna agreed that only a man who would bind himself wholeheartedly to her would do. That's when Shelly said, "Jenna, I've found him, and he's yours to embrace as well. You've seen me living with you as he began to change my affections. Jenna, no person knows me quite as well as you do. The transformation of my life goes back to my giving myself heart and soul to Jesus, who has given his heart and soul to me."

"Any chance you might be interested?"

End Notes

[i] Greg Ogden, *Transforming Discipleship*. Downers Grove: Intervarsity Press. 2003. p. 43-44.

[ii] "The Evangelical Scandal," *Christianity Today*, April 13, 2005.

[iii] I am indebted to Professor John H. Sailhamer who conveyed this interpretation to me while a student at Trinity Evangelical Divinity School on February 21, 1984 in a course on Poetry and Post-Exilic History.

[iv] Tim Chester and Steve Timmins, *Total Church: A Radical Reshaping around Gospel and Community*, Crossway, Wheaton, 2008, p. 170.

[v] Nicholas Thomas Wright, *Simply Christian*, SPCK: London, 2006, p. 138.

[vi] Dallas Willard, *The Great Omission: Reclaiming Jesus's Essential Teachings on Discipleship*. San Francisco: Harper. 2006. P. 61.

[vii] Robert Robinson, Come Thou Font of Every Blessing, 1758 Public Domain.